Lost Places, Hidden Treasures

Rare Photographs of Helena, Montana

by Ellen Baumler, Dave Shors,
Montana Historical Society, Independent Record

FARCOUNTRY
PRESS

Acknowledgments

It takes considerable talent to compile a project like *Lost Places, Hidden Treasures*.

First, we'd like to thank *Independent Record* Publisher Brad Hurd and Montana Historical Society Director Arnold Olsen for their direction and support of this project.

We sincerely appreciate the enthusiasm, professional skills and knowledge graciously shared by Delores (Lory) Morrow, Rebecca Kohl and Dianne Keller of the Montana Historical Society Photograph Archives; Jerry Cooper and Tom Ferris, photographers; Charlene Porsild, Library and Archives Program Manager; and Clark Whitehorn, Publications Program Manager.

At the *Independent Record*, we'd like to thank photographers George Lane and Jon Ebelt. Thanks also to Jeff Morrison and Crystal Wong Shors for sharing their special photographs, to Bob Smith at Farcountry Press for his excellent guidance and layout skills and to Barbara Fifer at Farcountry for her editing skills.

Front cover image: **See page 106.**

Title page: **Main Street looking north circa 1904 shows technological progress in the elaborate electrical system, powered from the Electric Block at Park and Sixth avenues, that cluttered downtown streetscapes.**
(Montana Historical Society Helena Uncatalogued Collection)

Back cover image: **A series of devastating earthquakes in October 1935 displaced nearly 300 boys and girls at St. Joseph's Orphanage in the Helena Valley. L. H. Jorud photographed the poignant aftermath of the disaster on October 31, 1935, as Sister Adolph helped some of the smallest victims cope. Thanks to the influence of US Senator James E. Murray, the children soon moved to Boulder Hot Springs where they remained until repairs to the home were completed in 1937.**
(IR file photograph)

Table Of Contents

Marcus Lissner, proprietor of the International Hotel, had an indomitable spirit that inspired the early business community. He lost his hostelry to fire so many times in the 1860s and 1870s that it was locally known as "The Phoenix." Lissner's beautiful South-Central Helena home is a testament to his standing in the community. The Lissners had many children, and at least one daughter occupied the home until she was very elderly. The Lissner kitchen in 1985 revealed the innovative use of old and new side by side.
(Courtesy of State Historic Preservation Office)

Benjamin F. Potts served as territorial governor from 1877 to 1883. Upon the removal of the territorial capital from Virginia City to Helena in 1875, the governor built this home at 312 Ewing Street, a short stroll to the Capitol at Courthouse Square. The home stood until circa 1905 when the palatial home of C. B. Power took its place.

(W. H. Taylor photograph. 953-989)

Introduction

Gusting spring winds swirl along the east slope of the Continental Divide, carrying the dust of our history—the minute specks of red Kessler bricks crushed by wrecking balls of Urban Renewal, the charred particles of wood of buildings destroyed by fires that roared along Last Chance Gulch in the late 19th century.

If only the dust could whisper its secrets in our ears, tell us where it has been and what it has seen.

But, few links remain to the men and women who founded and built our community.

Among the most notable and descriptive are the photographs and historical notations protected in the Photo Archives of the Montana Historical Society. Those black-and-white images of centuries past speak in frozen moments, captured for all time in faces, buildings, clothing and settings.

The images confirm that our predecessors were much like you and me. They were vital, eccentric and energetic; they were members of bicycle, tennis and music clubs; they were business people attempting to carve out a living and lifestyle along the east slope of the Continental Divide. Their early entrepreneurial dreams were building blocks of our economic fiber.

Some of the most intriguing of those frontier entrepreneurs were the image seekers we call photographers. They balanced artists' temperaments with strength and determination as they traveled the West with large and cumbersome cameras and darkroom equipment in tow, often setting up studios along the way.

We know from his remarkable early Helena images of the Broadwater and the Gulch that F. Jay Haynes was a frequent Helena visitor. *Following the Frontier, with F. Jay Haynes* chronicles his life from his early professional days in Moorehead, Minnesota where he opened his first studio at the age of 23, to his appointment in 1880 as official photographer for the Northern Pacific Railroad. The book describes the challenges of a pioneer photographer. Often carrying large cameras, glass plates, chemicals and developing equipment packed on horseback, Haynes captured some of his most remarkable views in the most remote reaches of the west.

Other Montana and Helena photographers might lack the notoriety of Haynes, or Miles City's L.A. Huffman, but the images they left as legacies are just as fascinating.

The names of some—Train, Bundy, Ball, Culbertson, Taylor, Reinig and Jorud—are embossed on their photographs, and our history.

Edward Reinig, self portrait. (Montana Historical Society PAc 74-104.78N)

Their life stories are as intriguing as the history of this place. They were men and women tied to myriad ventures. Some tasted the rewards and pains of frontier life.

Others, like Madame M. A. Eckert, must have found life an unraveling ball of intrigue. One of Montana's first women photographers, she had already established a studio here when Edgar Horace Train and his wife, Phebe, came to Last Chance Gulch in 1866.

Madame Eckert's advertisement in an 1868 Helena directory noted her gallery, located at the corner of Main and Wood streets, had recently received "from the East the most approved instruments and chemicals for taking photographs and ambrotypes." From her studio located in the heart of Helena's red light district, she offered "pictures colored, in oil or water colors, in the highest style of the art." Of course, in the interest of earning any penny available, she also offered lessons on the piano, guitar and in oil painting and drawing.

Madame Eckert later was caught in a maze of personal intrigue; she confessed on her death bed to the murder of Helena grocer John Denn. Her part in Denn's murder in his basement in late October of 1879, however, was never proven.

While lying terminally ill with a heart condition she supposedly confided in a friend: "I went in the night to Denn, called him up, took a bottle. I went in the cellar with him and hit him a lick. I killed John Denn with a hatchet."

But discrepancies in her confession included the fact Denn

Hanging of Joseph Wilson and Arthur L. Compton, April 30, 1870.
(M. A. Eckert photograph, Montana Historical Society 948-121)

had been killed with a hammer. Also, her daughter Jessie claimed Madame Eckert had been assaulted with a hatchet several years earlier and had never been the same again.

Her life was as colorful as her depictions. She also was alarmingly candid in her advertisements. In one, she suggested that her work was of highest quality. If it was unacceptable to a patron, she noted, it was most likely caused by the unattractiveness of the subject.

She was known for taking some of the most gruesome photos of local historical events, like her famous view of the 1870 double hanging of Joe Wilson and Arthur Compton.

Edgar Horace Train, who arrived in Helena at about the same, took a more sedate approach to life. He and his wife were pillars of the community and were active in the first chapter of the Eastern Star here in 1875.

E.H. and Phebe, newlyweds of about a year, arrived at Last Chance Gulch on Sept. 3, 1866, with Phebe's parents, Mr. and Mrs. Dwight Goodell. After camping for the first two weeks near present-day Neill Avenue, the Goodells started a market garden near the junction of Oro Fino and Grizzly gulches. The Trains lived with her parents until 1867 when they bought a photo shop owned by a man named Douglass, located above the Cosmopolitan Hotel.

Phebe worked alongside her husband, retouching negatives. In those days before the advent of films, photographers had to be chemists as well, preparing their own plates and papers.

Early Helena fires in the late 1860s and early 1870s burned out the Train galleries twice and forced them to move several times before settling at the corner of Water and Cutler streets near their home. During the late 1860s Train traveled through Montana with his photo gallery. Then in 1876, he received a prize at the Philadelphia Exposition, one of the highlights of his photography career. That same year he sold his Helena gallery to brother-in-law Oliver C. Bundy, who had become his partner in the venture. Train tried other enterprises, including taking out a patent on a shoe hook and lacing system called the "Train Shoe-Lacing Stud." Then the Trains moved to the East for a short time before returning to Helena to open an assay office at the foot of Broadway. He's listed as the proprietor of the Utah Assay Office in an 1893 city director.

The Trains lived in Helena until their deaths, his in 1899 and Phebe's in 1936. Their daughter, Percy Train, was a member of the 10-person graduating class of Helena High on May 23, 1895.

An adventurer to the last, Phebe eventually "tried all modes of travel from the covered wagon to the automobile," an article in the May 26, 1929, *Helena Independent* notes. The article suggested it wouldn't have taken much persuasion to induce her to ride an air mail plane to trace the route of her family's early covered wagon migration across the Plains in 1860.

O. C. Bundy's interest in photography developed in the gold fields of California and then Idaho, where he experimented in the craft. Failing to strike it rich as a prospector, he also tried work as a watchmaker and jeweler.

His career in photography advanced considerably when he married Rhodina Train, the sister of E. H. Train, in 1869. The couple returned to Helena and then Virginia City, while he toured the state capturing views of Montana's notable landmarks and people. Then in 1876 the couple moved to Helena again, this time to take over operation of the Train studio.

In an 1882 advertisement, Bundy touted he was "prepared to do better work than was ever done in the territory." But he noted he would not work on Sundays: "Orders on Sundays declined," he said.

Bundy died at the age of 64 on December 10, 1891.

Other turn-of-the-century photographers whose work brings life to the dust of Helena's past include Samuel J. Culbertson, J. P. Ball, and W. H. Taylor. Bits and pieces about their lives can be found, but their true legacies lie in their early-day Helena images.

Culbertson's name is imprinted on photographs of many significant local events. A fascinating Culbertson image in this book depicts the consecration of the cornerstone of the Cathedral of St. Helena in 1908. Bishop Carroll is the center of attention. But the crowd surrounding the platform is alive with conversations and actions, frozen in time by the camera shutter. A woman in the foreground rearranges her hair; a policeman looks up through a line of finely dressed women; school children hoist banners; and altar boys listen intently to Bishop Carroll.

Culbertson, who died in 1926 at the age of 55, is also noted for panoramas that captured the industrialization of Helena at the turn of the century. He was a single man who lived in Helena for 20 years. His studio and home were in the Bailey building.

William Taylor died just three years later, two days after Christmas in 1929. An Englishman, Taylor became interested in photography in the mid-19th century and operated a studio in Minneapolis before he purchased a studio here in 1889.

He photographed many of Helena's early leaders; he also specialized in photographing mine and ranch properties of the area.

An 1895 story in the *Helena Herald* notes Taylor had on sale in his Helena studios "the photographs of four convicted murderers who were then confined in the country jail here."

His obituary in the Dec. 28, 1929, *Independent*, says his studio in the early days was a favorite meeting place for friends and cronies, including W.A. Clark, Marcus Daly, Nick Kessler and Col. Thomas Cruse.

J. P. Ball and his son, J. P. Ball, Jr., were among the nation's early African American photographers. Their work often reflects a fascination with the unusual. One photo in this book, credited to J. P. Ball and Son, depicts an eccentric of the time, D. J. Schraier, as he poses in front of his cabin on 300 S. Clore Street under a sign that advertises his services as a clairvoyant. City directories in the late 1890s describe Schraier as a clairvoyant and fortune teller. One has to wonder if Schraier had a premonition his image would represent a curiosity in this 21st Century book.

J. P. Ball, Jr., was the first editor of *Colored Citizen*, which made its debut in 1894, devoted to helping Helena win the Helena-Anaconda capital-city contest.

Ball believed the *Colored Citizen* and the Montana African American voters could obstruct the Anaconda Company's "iron claw of corporate infernalism which has always crushed out the black man from every factory and workshop."

At that time the paper estimated about 2,500 African

Americans lived in Montana, including 500 in Helena. Ball felt the population was large enough to help make Helena Montana's capital. The *Colored Citizen* stopped publishing when the objective was met.

As Helena entered the 20th century, the two photographers who made the greatest impact were probably Edward Reinig and Leslie Jorud. Reinig's collection, which was donated to the Historical Society by his niece, Blanche Judge, depicts Helena in its formative years. He operated a photography business from roughly 1906 until he became ill around 1940.

Old and new are side by side in this view of Sixth Avenue and Jackson Street in the 1890s. The "Practical Tinsmith" kept a portable anvil in front of his business in a log cabin at Sixth and Jackson while downtown Helena sprang up around it. The cabin, a remnant of mining camp days, along with board sidewalks and unpaved streets contrast sharply with Helena's cosmopolitan architecture.

(C. F. Pearis photograph. MHS Uncatalogued Helena Collection)

Described by Mrs. Judge as a small-statured, frail man who never married, he was often seen carrying his huge camera on his back. A Roman Catholic, he documented the life of the local Catholic community. His early glass plate negatives also captured construction of the Capitol and life at Fort Harrison.

He died at his home, 52 South Rodney, in December 1947 at the age of 68. In the last years of his life he devoted his time to the mining interests of his father, who died here in 1940.

Leslie H. Jorud was an enduring and respected lensman, but his most notable legacy might be the amazing collection of old photographs he accumulated.

Jorud's interest in collecting was spurred in 1929 when the *Saturday Evening Post* telegraphed him and gave him 12 days to compile "all the pictures you can get of the Vigilantes and their day." The pictures he found, with the help of the state historical librarian were used to illustrate the series called "Vigilante," which ran in the issues from February 23 to March 23, 1929.

Until that time Jorud had specialized in commercial and portrait work while employed at O'Conner Drug Store. In 1930 he opened the Jorud Photoshop, which he operated until 1947 when he started the Jorud Commercial Photoshop on Jackson Street. He ran that business until 1969.

Throughout his entire career Jorud remained fascinated by the work of Montana's early-day photographers, like Train. A 1944 article in the *Independent Record*, by veteran Montana journalist Duane W. Bowler notes an 1870 photograph of Main Street taken by Train was among Jorud's most prized images.

Train's work was extremely hard to find, even during Jorud's career. Fire continued to be Train's curse, even after his death. Hundreds of the Train Gallery's early negatives from the 1870s and 1880s, stored in an attic at the gallery, were lost in a small fire in 1928.

The Jorud collection grew to include pictures of Alder Gulch in 1865, scenes at Bannack, Boot Hill at Virginia City, Indian teepees at the foot of Mt. Helena, early schools and notable Montanans. Photographs of Samuel T. Hauser, X. Beidler, Col. Wilbur Fisk Sanders, Chief Joseph and Calamity Jane were in his collection, which grew to more than 600 historic images by the mid-1950s.

Jorud represented the epitome of the self-preserving nature of photographers, past and present. Almost all seem fascinated not only in seeing images born in their darkrooms, but also with the work created by their predecessors.

Without Jorud's sleuthing, important examples of

Montana's first Baptist congregation organized in Helena in 1880 with 21 members. In 1883, the Grand Lodge of Montana, AF&AM, conducted the ceremonial laying of the cornerstone for the church at Warren and Eighth Avenue. By its tenth anniversary in 1890, the congregation numbered 233. The quaint and lovely church appears today almost as it was in the 1880s.

(J. P. Ball photograph, Montana Historical Society PAc 92-21)

Montana's early photographic work would have been lost.

It's with deep gratitude we acknowledge the creativity of these early men and women, plus a score not mentioned here, but whose work survives in bits and pieces.

Their images used here capture some of the most unusual scenes of Helena at the turn of the century in a collection of *Lost Places, Hidden Treasures*. This book is not intended to present a comprehensive history of the notable people, places and events that have been documented many times in previous publications. Instead, its purpose is to enhance our understanding of local history by focusing on images and information not often seen or shared.

One can only imagine the darkrooms of our early photographers, mystical places during the moments their photographs came to life.

One minute the exposed film or paper lay submerged in developer. The next, shades of gray took shape beneath the ripples as chemicals danced across the surface in the shallow tray. Moments later, the images became statements of life, still delicate and unprotected. Other chemicals stopped the development and then fixed the images. With the right processes they became archival in quality, testimony for future generations. All the while the photographer hunched over a sink, squinted in the faint light of an amber or red safe light, watching his or her work come to life. Hundreds of images.

Hundreds of pieces of our lives, preserved as statements that will exist long after we've all turned to dust.

The Spirit Of Adventure

Transportation

The journey to Helena was a three or four day trip, but our mother, Derinda Jane (then in her teens), loved to make it with her father or her uncle. In later years, when we traveled the same road, first with horses and buggies and then by automobile, Mother would remark on the differences in the trips. She thought she was really moving with horses, and then by car, there was just no comparison. At 80 years of age, she wished that she could take the trip in a plane. (The spirit of adventure was not yet gone.) That mode of travel was not so common as it is today but we have been sorry that we did not make more effort to make that dream come true.

from *"The Forgotten Pioneers,"* unpublished reminiscence of Lulu Tuttle Wallin, daughter of Derinda Jane Butts Tuttle, whose father and uncle built Helena's Pioneer Cabin.

Above: As twilight spread over the Helena Valley during good weather from the mid-1860s to the 1880s, huge freight wagons like these, loaded with merchandise from distant places, and oxen temporarily free of their heavy burdens, covered the plain northeast of town. At dawn the freighters would hitch their wagons and lumber into Main Street to unload long-awaited goods.

(F. A. Greenleaf photograph, Montana Historical Society 957-872)

Left: Some drivers preferred mules because they were faster than horses or oxen. "They were our faithful servants and a surer means of livelihood than the elusive gold in the mines," wrote Mary Ronan, whose father, James Sheehan, freighted goods to Helena and Virginia City. Drivers often hitched several wagons together. This mule train delivered goods on Vawter Street.

(Montana Historical Society 957-874)

Stagecoach passengers traveling through remote places like Wolf Creek Canyon, pictured here, endured rough roads, choking dust, extremes of weather and uncomfortable seats in the mid-nineteenth century. In the mid-1860s, stage service from Helena to the nearest rail connection at Corinne, Utah, a distance of some 550 miles, took at least four and a half days of traveling day and night. A one-way fare cost $145. Each driver worked a shift of about fifty miles, and "swing stations" every ten to thirteen miles provided fresh horses.

(F. A. Greenleaf photograph, Montana Historical Society 952-940)

Service to Butte began in 1879 with stages running every other day. A one-way ticket cost $2. Others operated to destinations in all directions. Even though the advent of the railroad to Helena in 1883 replaced stage travel to some places, there were still nine daily horse-drawn stages like this one out of Helena in 1886.

(Montana Historical Society 952-942)

Stages Through The Canyon

Frances M. A. Roe wrote a lively account of a stage ride from Helena through the Prickly Pear Canyon in *Army Letters from an Officer's Wife*. She dreaded meeting an oncoming ox train on the very narrow, boulder-strewn road. Sure enough, they had not gone far when a huge freighter lumbered toward them. A sheer precipice dropped on one side and soared skyward on the other. It seemed a hopeless situation.

The driver barked, "Get the lady out!" Men from the freighters sidled over. With no words spoken, they knew exactly what to do. They lifted the stage—trunks and all—up, over, and onto some of the boulders and led the horses between others. The horses stood at the edge of the precipice without a twitch while three teams of eight yokes of oxen passed by. "It made me ill," Frances wrote, "to see the poor patient oxen straining and pulling up the grade those huge wagons so heavily loaded. The crunching and groaning of the wagons, rattling of the enormous cable chains, and the creaking of the heavy yokes of the oxen were awful sounds, and above all the came yells of the drivers, and the sharp, pistol-like reports of the long whips…." After the wagons passed, the men returned and matter-of-factly set the stage on the road. The process was repeated six or seven times as the stage traveled through the canyon.

Above: After the Northern Pacific came to Helena in 1883, branch lines spread to various points, including Rimini on November 30, 1886. The crew on Northern Pacific Locomotive #102 and its caboose paused for a photograph to commemorate the occasion.

(F. J. Haynes photograph, Haynes Foundation Collection H-1734)

Above: As other modes of transportation gradually replaced stage travel, passengers piled into the already cramped quarters and others walked along to experience the last runs along the various routes. Will Campbell sat next to the driver on the last stage through the Prickly Pear Canyon. (Montana Historical Society 952-938)

Right: Passengers piled on the stage in Helena in May 1901 for the last ride to Dillon. (Montana Historical Society 952-944)

Right: Teamsters were still a familiar sight on Helena streets in the 1910s. The Helena Merchants Delivery Company at 608 N. Main went through several owners between 1910 and 1917. Those associated with the business like R. C. Wallace and E. P. Bourne were also local grocers.
(Montana Historical Society PAc 80-27.f19)

Below: Teamster Lloyd Dougherty, pictured circa 1904, delivered Kessler beer from the turn of the century until 1915. The company had retired its teams and switched to the automobile by 1915 when Dougherty, delivering beer to East Helena, stalled at a railroad crossing. He was killed instantly when a train hit the vehicle.
(Edward Reinig photograph, Montana Historical Society 953-066)

Left: The Fashion Livery and Boarding Stable replaced the Holter brothers' longtime lumberyard on the corner of Lawrence and Fuller in 1898. The stable yielded to the automobile in 1916 and was a dealership until the 1990s. Pictured is the Studebaker dealership circa 1918. Housing several businesses in 2002, the building's heavy beam construction and remnants of the livery are still visible inside in its second-story loft.
(Edward Reinig photograph, Montana Historical Society PAc 74-104.232)

Below: In the early 1890s, Helena had an assortment of trolleys operating on electricity, steam and horsepower. Helenans complained bitterly about the small coal-burning "dummy engines" that pulled some of the cars. They sent dust into homes and frightened horses. The smoke from the engine billowed past the waiting room of the Helena Electric Railway Company, whose cleaner cars were much preferred.
(Montana Historical Society PAc 80-27.f11)

Right: Several of Helena's assorted street cars made the run to the Broadwater Hotel. In the 1890s, women in fancy hats, boys in knickers and men in three-piece suits dress in their Sunday best for an afternoon at the resort.

(Montana Historical Society PAc 80-27.f15)

Below: The Helena Light and Traction Company operated the "Big Open" to the Broadwater Hotel, photographed in front of the Natatorium circa 1908.

(Montana Historical Society 953-369)

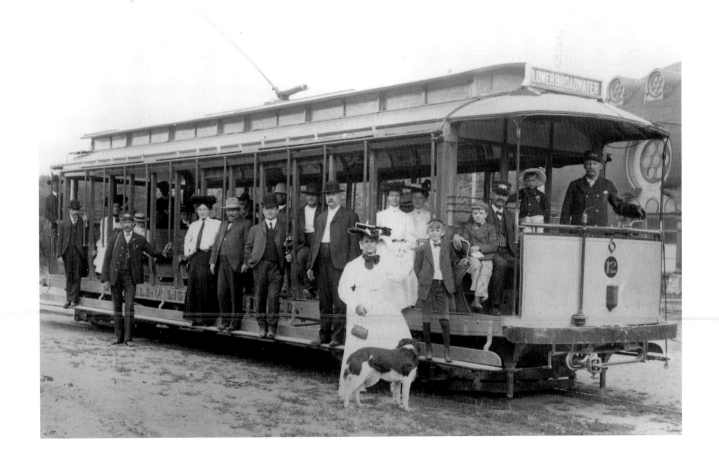

In this 1920 photograph Ed Follensby sits proudly in his airplane, the first owned in Helena. Follensby really propelled the local aviation movement. Its proud history includes fly-ins by Charles Lindbergh in 1927 and Amelia Earhart in 1933. In 1911, Cromwell Dixon was the first to fly across the Continental Divide in an airplane, leaving the fairgrounds in Helena and flying to Blossburg, just west of Priest Pass.

(Courtesy of Jeff Morrison)

R. E. "Red" Morrison founded Morrison Flying Service when he moved to Helena in 1931. His 1927 pilot's license was issued by the National Aeronautic Association and was signed by Orville Wright. "Red" was the first airport manager at the present airport and was both a state representative and a state senator. He resigned his senate seat in 1942 at the start of WWII when he went to Tampa, Florida to help train bomber pilots. He was killed in a crash of a Martin B-26 on Christmas Eve 1942, while in the U.S. Army Air Corps.

(Courtesy of Jeff Morrison)

Left: Helena's first airport was located at present-day Bill Roberts Golf Course when Charles Lindbergh flew the Spirit of St. Louis into Helena during his tour across America in 1927. The airport was moved to its present location in 1928. (Courtesy of Jeff Morrison)

Below: These two planes in front of Helena's original hangar at the present airport were owned by R. E. "Red" Morrison, founder of Morrison Flying Service. The picture, taken in 1931, shows a Lockheed Vega, 12B (numbered 12B because they didn't want to use the unlucky number 13 on an airplane) and a Fleet biplane.

(Courtesy of Jeff Morrison)

Above: In what is one of the first aerial photographs of Helena, the Lockheed Vega of R.E. "Red" Morrison is pictured flying over the Queen City. "Red" most likely was the pilot aboard the Vega, according to his son Jeff Morrison, and the photo was taken in 1932 by Leslie Jorud. (Photo courtesy of Jeff Morrison)

Left: The Mills family pioneered horticulture in Montana, founding the State Nursery in 1888. In the late 1930s, the company sported a thoroughly modern delivery van.

(Edward Reinig photograph, Montana Historical Society PAc 74-104.183)

Everything for Sale

Business and Industry

...fresh supplies of merchantable commodities fill not only the many stores, but scores of fire-proof warehouses besides. The main street of Helena seems to have everything for sale you could find in Philadelphia....

A.K. McClure,
Three Thousand Miles Through the Rocky Mountains, 1869.

Left: Local miners, like these photographed at a mining mill on Mount Helena, operated their claims along the Gulch. Mining produced a few millionaires and many legends including the one about Helena's hidden channel of gold. This especially persistent legend held that two prospectors on the run from Indians discovered an underground stream of rich gold deposits in 1863, a year before the Last Chance discovery men made their find. They marked the spot, but upon returning, could not locate it again.

(R. E. De Camp photograph,
Montana Historical Society PAc 95-61)

Below: The Porter Brothers operated this dredge north of Helena in the 1930s. Some claimed that the dredge cut into a deep, swiftly-flowing underground stream near Custer and Montana avenues and had to be cabled against the current. Others, however, disputed the tale. The river of gold to this day is a mystery.

(John L. Maloney photograph,
Montana Historical Society Mining Collection)

Horse-drawn conveyances and saddle horses for hire as well as boarding facilities and feed, were, like gas stations today, essential to every community in the nineteenth century. Thomas Sillers of Britt and Sillers Livery Stable was a longtime fixture, advertising the best horses and first-rate vehicles. (Montana Historical Society 953-134)

Edward Jezick operated a carriage works building and repairing horse-drawn vehicles.

(Montana Historical Society 953-082)

Building and heavy labor were still done by horses into the 1910s. Edward Reinig photographed men and horses making improvements to the Chessman Dam.

(Montana Historical Society PAc 74-104.321)

Left: Brewing was also an essential industry in mining camps and Helena had several breweries. Charles Beehrer established the first in 1864 west of town. Nicholas Kessler bought into the operation in 1865, becoming sole proprietor in 1868. Kessler rebuilt the brewery several times. The complex pictured, designed by well-known Helena architect T. F. Mathias in 1886 and photographed in 1908, stands today.
(S. J. Culbertson photograph, Montana Historical Society 953-051)

Below: Drivers delivered Kessler beer to the many saloons all over town, and shipped it on the railroad throughout the region. This driver, wagon loaded with kegs, paused for a photograph in front of the old Northern Pacific depot circa 1890.

(Montana Historical Society PAc 94-75.f11)

Above: **Kessler workers pose in front of the brewery circa 1890.**
(Montana Historical Society 953-063)

Right: **Kessler's 1886 plant was state-of-the-art with the first refrigeration system in Montana. A carbonic acid gas machine built in Germany by Frederick Krupp, the famous gun maker, powered the equipment. It was first of its kind used in a brewery in the United States. The photo dates to circa 1890.**
(Montana Historical Society 953-060)

Top: Helena had several brickyards by 1867 including one operated by Nick Kessler. In 1885 Kessler bought C. C. Thurston's brickworks, now the site of the Archie Bray Foundation. Oxen and horses supplied the power to mix the clay, and the bricks were molded by hand. (Montana Historical Society 953-071)

Above: Lime kilns were essential in producing the mortar for building with stone and brick. There is plenty of evidence of this early industry in the abandoned lime kilns south of town. (Dave Shors photograph)

Left: Grocer Michael Reinig's long career in Helena began as a baker in the gold camp. He branched out into groceries, an exacting business in the early days since an entire year's worth of goods, freighted by steamboat to Fort Benton and overland to Helena, had to be purchased all at once in amounts carefully estimated. Reinig later advertised with the motto "Where the dollar does its duty." The company's standard bearer, wearing coffee bean garments, photographed by the Taylor Studio, was a familiar regional image. (Montana Historical Society 953-118)

Right: Coffee roasting became a major focus of the Reinig Company early on. Green coffee, shipped from South America, was roasted in Reinig's plant at State and Joliet streets. After Michael Reinig's death in 1909, the business continued to be family operated. This 1914 display features a special blend of coffee Reinig's provided for the Weiss Café, a longtime Helena restaurant. (Edward Reinig photograph, Montana Historical Society 953-115)

Below: From Broadwater Hotel waiter to wealthy philanthropist, J. E. "Eddy" O'Connell was a self-made man who made Eddy's Bread a household word. Eddy's steam bakery and offices were at 18 Edwards Street from 1916 to 1972. A chain of 21 stores across the Northwest included a cake bakery at 40 S. Park Avenue, opened in 1928 in response to a new market for soft cake products.

(Edward Reinig photograph, Montana Historical Society PAc 74-104.115)

Lime Burning

The *Helena Weekly Independent* explained the lime industry in an article on January 19, 1884. Half a mile up Grizzly Gulch is "the place where all the lime for all the region hereabouts is (or has been until recently) quarried and burned." Two kilns ran at full capacity and several others on both sides of the roadway were under construction at that time. Manufacture of lime entailed quarrying and blasting the limestone from the cliff behind. Handcars ran on a track for conveying the stone or it was tumbled down the embankment to the tops of the kilns where the limestone chunks were dumped into the huge chimneys. A roaring fire of pine in the furnace at the bottom of the kiln burned continuously for several days and nights. After the lime had burned sufficiently, workers shoveled the powdered substance out into the "room" at the base of the kiln where it could be loaded onto wagons and hauled to building sites.

Above: The New York Store, founded in the 1880s, was a fixture along North Main Street for more than half a century. Family-owned and operated until the 1960s, this display circa 1920 is typical of the store's artistic window dressings.

(Edward Reinig photograph, Montana Historical Society PAc 74-104.182)

Above: The New York Store perished in the 1928 fire. Rebuilt and renamed Fligelman's Department Store, the new building's architectural features include a charming tailor and seamstress to remind the community of this pioneer family's excellent clothing business.

(Courtesy State Historic Preservation Office)

Below: The ladies' millinery on the second floor of the New York Store offered elegant counters, display cases, and mirrored vanities for trying on the latest fashions.

(Edward Reinig photograph, Montana Historical Society PAc 74-104.171)

Right: Butchers and grocers proudly pose around counters at the Union Market, 6th and Jackson, a prosperous Helena grocery store for almost a century. Pictured from left to right are Albert Nagy, Fred G. Zimmerman Sr., Adolf Neuser, Harry Reichter (owner), the office lady and two unidentified deliverymen, unknown grocer, Warren Elliott, Wesley Hart and Lewellyn Reichter. Fred DeWolf, Sr., purchased the Union in 1943 and his sons, Fred, Bill, and George, went to work at the market when they returned from WWII. The DeWolf family ran the store until 1986, and the Union Market finally closed its doors in 1990.
(Edward Reinig photograph, Montana Historical Society PAc 74-104.107)

Below: Helena had no lack of butchers, meat markets, and slaughterhouses (called "abattoirs" in the nineteenth century). (Montana Historical Society PAc 94-75.f11)

The Kain Granite Company, one of Helena's several stone quarrying operations, was active from the mid-1890s to the 1920s supplying local stone for buildings, including that used for the State Capitol's wings in 1910. The company's office at Seventh and Jackson, built in 1912, is a fine example of their work. This photograph dates from circa 1915.

(Edward Reinig photograph, Montana Historical Society PAc 74-104.316)

The manufacture of rugs was an unusual industry that endured in Helena for several decades. Schneider & Son's Helena Rug Factory boasted the largest "fluff rug" operation in Montana, shown here at 1040 Helena Avenue in 1915. From the 1920s to about 1933, the factory operated in the old Northern Pacific Depot, which had been moved to 1330 Lyndale Avenue.

(Montana Historical Society PAc 94-75.f11)

Pharmacist John Horsky advertised that his East Side Drug Store was the "only pharmacy in the City with a fresh, up-to-date stock of drugs and drug sundries." Horsky provided the central spittoons in an attempt to keep his floor clean. Despite "modern" electric lighting, a wood stove provided heat. (Montana Historical Society 953-099)

Right: Horsky's drug store at 204 N. Rodney was a familiar neighborhood fixture from about 1905 to 1918.
(Montana Historical Society 953-098)

Below: Vicenzo and Anna Marino, and later their daughter Sophia Cavallari, ran a grocery business that endured from the mid-1910s to 1971. Pictured circa 1914 in their first location on South Main Street, the Marinos soon moved to the Parchen Block on Broadway where the family lived and kept lodging rooms above the store.
(Montana Historical Society 953-109)

In 1892 a representative of the American Biscuit and Manufacturing Company came to Helena and selected a building site two blocks east of Helena Avenue on Boulder Avenue. The contract was let to George S. Appleton, who also drew the plans, to construct the three-story cracker factory for $16,562.80. By 1908, the National Biscuit Company operated the plant and employed 150 workers and nine traveling salesmen. Mae Gooch, Disa Williams and Miss Turner sit on a fence outside their workplace in this undated photograph.

(Montana Historical Society PAc 94-75.f18)

The National Biscuit Company boasted fifty thousand feet of floor space for the manufacture of crackers and candies that ranged from "stick type to the finest chocolates and cream goods." The work crew poses neatly in uniform outside the building on Boulder Avenue circa 1910.

(Montana Historical Society 953-037)

Agriculture was, and still is, a major local industry that has come a long way from the days of horse and plow. Edward Reinig photographed modern harvesting on the Colbenson Brothers' farm in the 1940s. (Montana Historical Society PAc 74-104.210)

Frank And Jovial Companionship

...with a red-faced, hard-swearing Montana stage-driver to point out its beauties and peculiarities, [and] I a dusty and battered traveler clinging to the top of an old Concord coach. Then it was that Helena made its strongest impression. ...It seemed then a wonder of eager, busy, money-getting and money-spending, far-Western life, hospitable, buoyant, extravagant, enterprising, and courageous. The men seemed a different stamp from those of the East—generous, hopeful, intensely in love with their free, wild mountain country and heartily fond of frank and jovial companionship.

E. V. Smalley,
The Northwest Magazine, September 1890

Masons lay the cornerstone for the Masonic temple that once stood at Edwards and Main. Crowds throng on rooftops to witness the showy ritual on June 14, 1872. The Whitlatch Building marks the northeast corner of Jackson and Broadway where the Masons later built a larger building. The office of the Democratic *Rocky Mountain Gazette*, back center, operated from 1866 until it was lost to the great fire of January, 1874.

(E. H. Train photograph, Montana Historical Society PAc 80-27.f11)

Dubious Honor

Dr. L. Rodney Pococke, a graduate of a St. Louis medical school, was the first professional medical man to move to Helena permanently. He came, however, not to practice medicine but to combat his own tuberculosis. Pococke hoped the mountain climate would benefit his deteriorating health. Little did he know that Montana winters were harsh, and accommodations primitive. After living in a badly-chinked log cabin for several months where the wind blew over him at night and snow had settled on his bedding in the morning, Dr. Pococke's tenuous health failed and he died in the spring of 1865. His was the mining camp's first death. An elaborate Masonic funeral was arranged according to Dr. Pococke's last request, precipitating the first meeting of Masons in Helena. Nearly every resident witnessed the funeral procession, and for the dubious distinction of being the first to go, a street was named in honor of the doctor. Helena has no Pococke Street; residents wouldn't go quite that far. Instead, it is Rodney Street that serves as a tribute to Dr. L. Rodney Pococke. Although Rodney wasn't even his first name, it's the thought that counts.

Right: In the 1890s long-distance cycling was the craze of the day. An 1892 *Herald* noted Helena "wheelmen" turned out to welcome a New York City man who was touring the world on a cycle. In this picture, George Gilpatrick and his partner prepare to ride to Chicago in 1893, bound for the World's Fair. Members of the Helena Bicycle Club pose in the background.
(Montana Historical Society 953-289)

Below: The Society of Montana Pioneers organized in 1884. Those in residence or en route to Montana on or before May 26, 1864—the date Montana Territory was created—were eligible for membership. The Sons and Daughters of Montana Pioneers organized in 1892. The two groups built a cabin in the spirited tradition of those who had firsthand experience in log construction. However, this turn-of-the-century shelter was at the Montana State Fairgrounds and used as a "rest tent."
(Edward Reinig photograph, Montana Historical Society PAc 74-104.244)

Members of the Helena Woodmen Drill Team pose trim and proper in this 1909 photograph by Edward Reinig. (Montana Historical Society 953-311)

Helena's first tennis club was organized in July 1888. The club had "grounds" on the west side and was scheduled to begin the season's sport in July of that year. This picture shows club members in the 1890s. City and state tournaments held in the mid-1890s were two to three weeks in duration.

(Montana Historical Society 953-310)

Members of the Helena Rod and Gun Club pose in this early photo. (Montana Historical Society 953-309)

Right: **For well over a century Helenans have had a keen interest in baseball. The Helena Merchants gathered for a team photo at Scullen Field, which was located on the north end of the Carroll campus. An independent, semi-pro team, the Merchants would pass the hat at games to collect enough money for equipment and travel expenses.**

(Montana Historical Society PAc 94-75.f1)

Below: **Players for the Webster Cigars pose in front of Bryant School in the 1920s.**

(Montana Historical Society PAc 94-75.f1)

The German community organized the Helena Turnverein, or Athletic Club, in 1892 and built Turnhalle (Turner Hall) at Warren and Helena Avenue. The club promoted weekly boxing matches held in the new facility's arena. In 1901, the building with its spacious gymnasium became University Hall housing the president's office and classrooms for Montana Wesleyan University. Long familiar as Helena Body and Paint, the building's automobile affiliation began by the 1920s as Floyd Howe's Midway Garage and Auto Transfer.

(H. J. Lowry photograph, Montana Historical Society PAc 80-27.f10)

Members of the Montana Volunteer Infantry gather at Camp Robert B. Smith at Helena in May, 1898, under Col. Harry C. Kessler, commanding officer. Called to action by Gov. Robert Smith, the First Montana was mustered into the U.S. Army on May 9. It left Helena on May 25, trained in San Francisco and then boarded the S.S. *Pennsylvania* on its way to the Philippines, arriving on August 24 with a strength of 1,015 men. The first casualty list from the Philippines showed two killed and 34 wounded from the First Montana, including several Helena men. (J. P. Ball & Son photograph, Montana Historical Society PAc 88-39)

Fort Harrison

The meeting of the Great Northern and Northern Pacific lines was strategic in placing Fort Benjamin Harrison at Helena in 1892. The installation was named after the 23rd president of the United States (1889-1893). Harrison's son, Russell, had served a term as head of Helena's federal assay office in the 1880s. The post, however, was renamed Fort William Henry Harrison in honor of Benjamin's grandfather, the 9th president of the United States. By 1897 the expansion of facilities included $36,000 for a bachelors' officers quarters for four officers, a double set of non-commissioned officers' quarters, and barracks for a band. That year Company D of the 25th Infantry held a special New Year's Eve ball and open house. The 25th Infantry orchestra supplied the music for dancing. The quarters were draped with flags and the evening's centerpiece was a picture of Custer's Last Charge decorated with roses and carnations.

The fort remained an active army post until 1913. With the U.S. involvement in WWI, the Montana Regiment of the National Guard assembled at Fort Harrison in 1917 and, in 1919, the U.S. Public Health Service took over management of the fort. At the start of WWII, President Franklin D. Roosevelt activated the First Special Service Force, an elite group of Canadian and American Army personnel. After training at Fort Harrison, the force served with distinction in the both the Pacific and European theaters.

Fort Harrison today is the site of the Veterans Affairs Medical and Regional Office Center, providing medical care to veterans of all branches of the service.

Crowds lined both sides of the street to say goodbye to Company C— 163rd Montana Infantry Regiment on October 24, 1917 as soldiers departed for France during WWI. Created to fight in the war, the 163rd was the figurehead of the Montana National Guard for some 80 years. Of the 1,539 soldiers who fought in World War I, 91 were killed in combat and another 308 were injured. After returning from the war, the 163rd constituted the majority of the Montana National Guard until it was again activated to serve in World War II. On Sept. 16, 1940 a total of 119 officers, one warrant officer and 1,631 enlisted men reported to armories throughout Montana for what they were told would be a one-year support effort. The Japanese attack on Pearl Harbor extended the unit's activation indefinitely and members served proudly and strategically in key battles throughout the war effort. Gen. Douglas MacArthur said of the unit, "I have the greatest affection and admiration for the 163rd Infantry Regiment from Montana."

(Above, Edward Reinig photograph, Montana Historical Society 953-639 and below, L. H. Jorud photograph, Montana Historical Society 953-646)

First Born And Best Loved

Public Services and Spaces

Already the old edifice is dismantled and soon the place that knew it will know it no more. Goodbye, old friend, goodbye. But thou cannot perish! The wreath of immortality is on thy brow. As long as Montana shall live, thy name and fame will endure. As long as these rock-ribbed mountains shall hold the world together, thou shalt not perish. This new structure of grandeur and beauty is but thy child, thy first born and best loved..."

Chief Justice Decius S. Wade upon the dedication of the Lewis and Clark County Courthouse, July 1, 1887.

Right: Postmaster John Patten poses with a sack of mail delivered by stage in December 1866 at the Helena Post Office on Broadway. A false front covers the simple log building. First generation buildings sported false fronts to make them appear larger and taller, giving residents a sense of security in isolated frontier communities.

(Montana Historical Society 953-887)

Below: On July 1, 1887, the post office inaugurated free postal delivery to the homes of Helena residents. "Gray-coated letter carriers" became a familiar sight on city streets. By the early 1900s, Helena's mail service was motorized.

(Montana Historical Society 953-901)

Helena's Public Auditorium at Seventh and Warren next door to Central School was long a hub of the community. Gala parades like the one pictured frequently ended with a public address in the auditorium. The 2,500-seat facility also served a variety of community functions. In 1899, it hosted a welcome home banquet for Company L of the First Montana Volunteers returning from the Philippines. In 1900, it held the widely attended funeral of Colonel Robert Bruce Wallace of the 37th Volunteer Infantry who was wounded in the Philippines and later died of complications from a bullet in his lung. (Montana Historical Society 953-571)

In the early twentieth century, flower shows in Helena were popular and elaborate, transforming the Public Auditorium into a bower of springtime blooms. (S. J. Culbertson photograph, Montana Historical Society 953-516)

The 2,500 volumes of Helena's first library, founded in 1868, were lost in the fire of 1874. By 1892 when the library moved into the new quarters it shared with the Public Auditorium, its inventory included 10,000 volumes. In 1895 there were 90 periodicals published in Montana and all could be found in the library's reading room, shown here in 1897.

(Montana Historical Society 953-587)

Right: Amid the tailings of early-day placer mining, the cornerstone of St. Peter's Hospital was laid in June 1887 at the corner of present-day 11th Avenue between Logan and Cruse Avenue. Although this photo was taken in the mid-1890s, the barren landscape appears to have been recently "dug on." Tailings like these remained for decades as a reminder that mining gave the town its start. (Montana Historical Society 953-531)

Center: Rev. F. T. Webb, of the Episcopal Church, founded St. Peter's Hospital in the early 1880s and first located it near the Northern Pacific depot. In 1885 the hospital moved to the former A. M. Holter residence on Jackson Street. Once the 11th Avenue facility was completed, nurses were in residence on the third floor. In 1908, St. Peter's advertised its services as "absolutely unsectarian and humanitarian." From 1918 to the 1920s, the hospital also operated a school of nursing. Edward Reinig photographed St. Peter's nurses circa 1905. (Montana Historical Society PAc 74-104.309)

Below: Aid to the indigent has been part of Lewis and Clark County services since the founding of a miner's hospital in 1866. The hospital moved to 160 acres in the Helena Valley in 1870. The facility pictured was built in 1885, enlarged in 1899, and in use until 1935 earthquakes destroyed it. The hospital rebuilt. It was the forerunner of the Cooney Convalescent Home, named after longtime physician and public health advocate Dr. Sid Cooney. Its successor is now located on East Broadway near the current St. Peter's Hospital. (Montana Historical Society PAc 80-27.f10)

Lost Places, Hidden Treasures

Left: The Odd Fellows Home on Head Lane in the West Prickly Pear Valley at its dedication, October 17, 1910, brought a needed service to the valley. The facility housed both children and adults of the Order who needed a home.
(Montana Historical Society 953-322)

Below: On January 26, 1926, Home residents included 10 children and 15 elderly adults. Fire broke out in the third floor ceiling and quickly spread, destroying this facility. High school student B. Murrel "Smokey" Kratzer, who lived at the home with his siblings, was a hero, rescuing several residents. No one was injured and the home, now the Mountain Meadow Inn, was promptly rebuilt.

(S. J. Culbertson photograph, Montana Historical Society 953-323)

The Lewis and Clark County Courthouse, a significant and often overlooked landmark, illustrates the architectural diversity the railroad made possible. The distinctive stone trim is brownstone shipped by rail from Bayfield, Wisconsin. In 1887 the grand new building replaced the 1867 stone courthouse, on the right in this picture. Stone from the old building was reused in the terrace wall that borders the grounds. The courthouse served as territorial capitol and, upon statehood in 1889, it served as Montana's State Capitol until 1902. Earthquakes necessitated removal of its clock tower, but the building continues to serve Lewis and Clark County.

(Montana Historical Society 953-344)

🔖 Lewis and Clark County 🔖

On a scroll at the north entrance of the courthouse is the name "Lewis and Clarke County." Originally named Edgerton County after Montana Territory's first governor, Sidney Edgerton, the county name was changed to Lewis and Clarke County to honor the explorers. It is the only county so named in the United States. However, questions soon arose over the spelling of William Clark's name. Our forebears often spelled their own names in various ways, and Clark's was spelled both with and without the final "e," so which one was correct became a matter of concern. In 1900, Montana Historical Society librarian Laura E. Howey's research into the matter ended the controversy. According to the War Department in Washington, D.C., the U.S. Senate's nomination of Captain Clark as a military officer had no final "e." Further, as Governor of Missouri, his name had been spelled Clark. And, publication of Lewis and Clark's journals, which in the original included both spellings, regularized the name to Clark. An act of the legislature allowed dropping the archaic "e" and the official spelling became Lewis and Clark County, but the memory of the older spelling remains on the courthouse scroll.

Above: Courthouse Square in the 1890s boasted the state capitol and a new county jail. Change was imminent, however, as the old Presbyterian Church (demolished in 1900) in the right corner stood empty while an unsightly warehouse sported billboards on all sides. A horse corral behind served the adjacent livery stable. The tower on the home of prominent pioneer attorney Cornelius Hedges is visible left of the jail. That home still stands on the corner of Broadway and Rodney, minus its tower.
(C. F. Pearis photograph,
Montana Historical Society 953-352)

Left: The fortress-like appearance of the Lewis and Clark County Jail, completed in 1892, proclaims its somber function. Inside, jailor and deputy sheriff Dougal "Duke" McGregor sits at his desk, in 1916 where he can keep an eye on prisoners in the cage at left. The former jail now houses the Myrna Loy Center for the Performing Arts.
(Montana Historical Society 953-561)

Right: Ghost signs like this one on the livery stable once serving Courthouse Square are treasured remnants that recall the early days.
(Dave Shors photograph)

Below: Officials moved into the new House of State in 1902, the first capitol building in the nation to be wired for electricity. The Capitol Rotunda, pictured in 1903, appears as it does today after extensive restorations were completed in time for its 100th birthday.
(Montana Historical Society 952-844)

A Longing For Home

Neighborhoods

"... it was my privilege to journey around this beautiful world. There was no spot where I wished to linger. There was always a longing in my heart to be at home. ...

from the unpublished memoirs of
Sallie Davenport Davidson, early Helena pioneer.

D. J. Miller, John Cowan, Reginald Stanley and John Crabb made a lucky strike near the northeast corner of present-day Park Avenue and Wall Street on July 14, 1864. The discoverers were dubbed the Four Georgians, but only Cowan was from Georgia. A few decades later no one remembered why they had been so named. One theory is that the discoverers were using the "Georgian method" of mining. Georgia was a major gold producer before the western gold rushes. If this photograph of placer miners Jerry Robinson (left) and Ike Newcomer (right) looks familiar, it should. Taken in Blue Cloud Gulch west of Helena, it was the model for the large oil painting that hangs in the Senate Chamber of the State Capitol. At the age of 19 Robinson came to Montana from Virginia and started mining in Nelson Gulch west of Helena.

(Montana Historical Society 958-350/359)

The gold rushes displaced native peoples and changed the landscape. Indians remained in the Prickly Pear Valley for a time near the placer diggings, quietly observing. Legend has it that Tomah was a chief who watched the miners destroy his homeland. Some proposed the name Tomah instead of Helena (a town in Scott County, Minnesota). As late as 1874, Bundy and Train photographed these lodges northwest of town with Mount Helena in the background.

(Montana Historical Society 953-370)

Above and right: Miners' cabins along present-day South Park Avenue like the Pioneer Cabin comprised the camp's first neighborhood. The cabin, now a museum, is Helena's oldest documented dwelling, constructed in two stages in 1864 and 1865. Sallie Davenport Davidson, who lived next door, recalled living under a sod roof, "...at the first heavy rain, there was not a dry spot in the house, and when that dirt was thoroughly soaked, it would drip for days...." (Above, Montana Historical Society 953-129, right, Dave Shors photograph)

Left: Some moved on and others who stayed built more comfortable housing away from the diggings. William Parkinson built Helena's first frame home in 1865 on Pine Street. The home's appearance today still resembles this Taylor Studio photograph.

(Montana Historical Society 954-136)

Above: By 1870 Helena's population was roughly 3,000. A Chinese community of some 600 citizens operated small businesses, provided services and paid their taxes. Urban renewal in the 1970s erased all remnants of this important ethnic group. The cabin at 300 S. Park Street at the foot of Reeder's Alley is the only exception. (Montana Historical Society PAc 80-27.f15)

Right: J. P. Ball photographed Daniel J. Schraier beneath his shingle in front of the same one-room cabin at 300 S. Park in 1899. At various times during the decade Schraier listed his occupation as clairvoyant or fortuneteller. Schraier was a longtime neighbor who previously occupied one of the tiny apartments of Reeder's Alley. Louis Reeder, a Pennsylvania brick and stone mason, built his apartment complex in the 1870s and early 1880s. Reeder's Alley offered miners more comfortable housing than the log cabins along the gulch. The few surviving cabins and alley comprise Helena's oldest intact territorial period neighborhood. (Crystal Wong Shors collection)

Below: In 1890 Chinese proprietors operated 28 laundries in Helena. Professional offices as well as dry goods stores, groceries and restaurants crowded into the community at the south end of the gulch. Few Chinese families remained in Helena after the 1920s, but landmarks like this Chinese Masonic Hall at 308 West Main recalled their contributions to the early community. (Montana Historical Society 953-317)

Above: Chinese workers made tremendous contributions toward Montana's progress, helping to lay the tracks of the Northern Pacific across Montana in the 1880s and building the Mullan Tunnel across the Great Divide. Chinese in Helena were especially important to the early community for the gardens they cultivated south of the gulch, and the produce they sold locally. "Ling," posing in the garden of Mrs. John Ming in 1891, worked as a cook. (Montana Historical Society 940-902)

Below: Quang Fang Low operated his business in the 1890s at 206 West Main next to the old city hall. (Montana Historical Society 953-083)

In 1894 the newly completed Howie Street Bridge (also called the Morelli Bridge after Charles Morelli, the mason who did the stone work), far left, allowed development above Reeder's Alley and provided the first access over "Reeder's Gulch." (Montana Historical Society PAc 80-27.f14)

Saving the Alley

George Mitchell, the last resident of the Pioneer Cabin, operated a wood business and raised chickens in his backyard from circa 1903 until his death in 1938. Mitchell had no heirs and so the cabin and nine adjacent lots, valued at $450, were slated for public auction. A group of farsighted citizens recognized the cabin's historic importance and raised enough by public subscription to purchase the property, thereby inaugurating one of the first preservation efforts in the West. After they refurbished and furnished it with period items, some of them original to the cabin, the Last Chance Gulch Restoration Association opened the cabin to the public in July 1939 and still maintains it.

Behind the Pioneer Cabin, Reeder's Alley winds upward along West Cutler Street. Into the 1950s, its tiny apartments housed single pensioners. Derelict and falling into ruin, the alley was slated for demolition. Three spirited Helenans—Pat Boedecker, Eileen Harper, and Jane Tobin—set their minds to saving this slice of early Helena. The three women purchased one building, cleaned it up, and after Reeder's Alley owners George Sullivan and Reed Matthews relocated their 23 tenants, the women bought the rest of the alley, too. They converted the rooms into artists' galleries and shops. Several owners later in 2001 Kathy and Darrell Gustin donated Reeder's Alley to the State of Montana.

Jesuit priests built Helena's first Catholic church atop a gentle rise in 1866, predicting that "this rocky hill will blossom like a garden." The Sisters of Charity of Leavenworth, Kansas arrived in 1869 to help transform the barren hilltop into a complex of institutions known as Catholic Hill. The three homes pictured in the foreground circa 1890 still stand on Broadway. Behind left to right are St. Vincent's Academy for Girls, Cathedral of the Sacred Hearts of Jesus and Mary, the bishop's residence (later St. Ann's Infants' Home) and St. John's Hospital. The Herrmann Furniture Company is the building at the right edge.

(Montana Historical Society PAc 80-27.f14)

In the early 1870s, the Cathedral of the Sacred Hearts of Jesus and Mary replaced the first simple frame church. After St. Helena Cathedral held its first services in December 1914, Sacred Hearts sat abandoned and was demolished in the 1920s.

(Edward Reinig photograph, Montana Historical Society PAc-74-104.286)

Right: The only survivors after earthquakes devastated Catholic Hill in 1935 were the St. John's Hospital laundry facility and St. Aloysius Boys' School (now known as Immaculata Hall), left pictured circa 1930. St. John's was rebuilt on the site of St. Vincent's across Ewing Street in 1939.
(Montana Historical Society PAc 74-104.264)

Below: Three Sisters of Charity pose with Dr. William L. Steele and others in front of St. John's Hospital in 1897. Dr. Steele, known as the "grand old man of medicine," won renown as a surgeon after the Battle of the Big Hole in 1877. Dr. Steele's diverse career included service as county sheriff and treasurer, ten years as coroner, three terms as mayor, and as a state legislator.
(Montana Historical Society 953-522)

Arrival of the Northern Pacific in 1883 meant for Helena "virtual annexation to the United States." A new commercial area quickly sprang up near the depot. Alexander Beattie, one of the first depot district developers, built the Grand Pacific Hotel (the building with the many chimneys) for $3,000 in 1883. By 1891 it had been revamped with the latest hot water heaters, electric lights, and an all-night cook. Passengers in this 1885 photo wait at the depot.

(Haynes Foundation Collection H-1570)

Above: Brightly painted horse-drawn trolleys took the first train travelers "up town" for ten cents. Much later, motorized cabs took over this service. The City Cab Company made frequent trips to and from the business district. Harry Bouchet, parked in front of Union Station, is at the wheel with Ed Jezick in the front seat and Bill Gabel in the back seat, far left. (Montana Historical Society 953-383)

Left: By 1890, 22 passenger trains stopped in Helena and the original frame station was woefully inadequate. Long-term plans for a new depot reached fruition in 1904. Charles A. Reed of the firm Reed and Stem designed Helena's Union Station, pictured, as well as other depots across Montana. The firm later supplied the engineering specifications for New York's famed Grand Central Station. (Dave Shors photograph)

Right: H. Walter Larson came from Sweden to join relatives in the Sixth Ward in 1902. Larson founded the Northern Pacific Meat Company in 1906 with a capital investment of $145. His most valuable piece of equipment was a $40 horse. Larson rented this frame storefront, on the present-day site of Beattie Memorial Park, for $5 a month. Two pounds of round steak then cost 25¢; pork chops were 12½¢ a pound.

(Montana Historical Society PAc 94-75.f5)

Left: In 1912, Larson renamed and expanded his business, moving it across the street. Pictured in its second location circa 1917, the Montana Meat Company did business in the depot district until 1973.

(Montana Historical Society PAc 94-75.fl7)

Right: Left to right on Railroad Avenue are the Capital Hotel, a single family residence, and the German Café and Boardinghouse run by the James German family. The small brick home, remodeled in the 1890s and still standing today, was a public wash house in the 1880s. The bustling depot district gave travelers their first impressions of Helena, yet there were no streetlights and no sidewalks until after 1906. The city slowly improved the area, finally paving the streets with brick in 1915. Sidewalks and streetlights but no paving date this photo as post-1906 and pre-1915.

(Montana Historical Society PAc 94-75.fl1)

Top and above: The table is set for dinner at a Lyndale Avenue boarding-house circa 1904. Railroad workers and shop employees who worked in the small businesses near the depot kept tables always full at mealtime. (Montana Historical Society PAc 74-95)

Left: St. Mary's Parish served Helena's working backbone in the Sixth Ward. In 1905, church services and a school taught by Sisters of Charity were conducted in the Knights of Pythias Hall and from 1908 to 1909, in this storefront at 1322 Gallatin. (Montana Historical Society 953-741)

Above: St. Mary's congregation stood at 500 when these children of the Sixth Ward celebrated their first communion circa 1909.

(Montana Historical Society PAc 74-361)

Right: St. Mary's Catholic Church and School at 1421 North Roberts, now Rocky Mountain Christian High School, was built to serve the Sixth Ward. Bishop John Patrick Carroll and Monsignor Victor Day are among the last in the processional at the dedication ceremonies in 1910.

(Montana Historical Society PAc 74-104.313)

Left: The Larson Block at 1400 Helena Avenue, built circa 1921 and several times remodeled, incorporated a number of businesses including H. Walter Larson's own meat market and Bud Ferrat's confectionery, established on the eve of Prohibition circa 1917. The Ferrats' children left to right are Toots, Vivian and Margaret with their parents. (Montana Historical Society PAc 94-75.f6)

Below: After Prohibition in 1933, Ferrat's ice cream parlor became Ferrat's Dance and Dine, where Helenans experienced their first curb service. Patrons lined up all around the block, tying up traffic to such an extent that Ferrat had to discontinue the experiment. (Montana Historical Society PAc 94-75.f6)

L. H. Jorud captured children enjoying the wading pool the city installed in Beattie Park. The city created the park in 1930 with a trust bequeathed by Anna and Mary Beattie of Rockford, Illinois, as a memorial to their brothers, Thomas, Alexander and George.

(Montana Historical Society PAc 94-75.f2)

Beattie Park was a vast improvement over the seedy and abandoned 1880s buildings that covered the block west of Union Station in 1929. The area had developed a reputation as the worst looking depot area on the entire NP route. The park, minus its wading pool and tile bench, is a "beauty spot" next to the tracks even today. (Montana Historical Society PAc 94-75)

The remnant brick street with a section of trolley tracks is the last of its kind in Helena and a reminder of the days when the depot district was a busy hub.

(Dave Shors photograph)

Golden Gizzards

Einar Larson, H. Walter's son, told about a grocer whose shop was near the railroad depot. The grocer's specialty was fresh dressed turkeys. His birds were shipped live by rail from some small Montana community. As time went by, this grocer began to notice something interesting as he butchered and dressed his turkeys. The turkeys came from an area that had been extensively placer mined, and the birds were pecking around in the tailings. The grocer came to realize that many of these birds had hidden treasures: their gizzards sometimes yielded gold nuggets. His customers seemed not to notice that their holiday turkeys were sometimes gizzardless. Over the years the grocer collected a huge jar of gold nuggets that he kept well-concealed in the basement. When the 1935 earthquakes struck, the depot area was especially hard hit, and this grocery collapsed in on itself, burying the jar of gold. The grocer not only lost his business, but his hoard of gold too, and to this day it lies buried somewhere near the depot.

Left: Family groceries dotted Helena's eastside neighborhoods. Walter Dorsey built up one of the most successful small businesses at 900 8th Avenue. He came to Helena in 1891, saved his money while he worked at the Montana Club and the Broadwater Hotel, and opened his first grocery in 1895. In 1899 he moved to this location. He and his wife, Almira, operated the store until 1907, when Dorsey succumbed to pneumonia. Almira, pictured with her daughter, continued the business until 1931. (Montana Historical Society PAc 2002-2)

Right: Walter Dorsey poses with his family in front of their 8th Avenue grocery prior to 1907. After 1931, the store under other owners served the neighborhood until the 1950s. Just behind and left of the store is St. Helena's Catholic Church. During the 1890s it offered Helena's only Catholic Mass said in the German language.

(Edward Reinig photograph, Montana Historical Society PAc 74-104.266)

Left: Churches in the neighborhood that illustrate Helena's cultural diversity included the St. James African Methodist Episcopal Church at 5th and Hoback, the Scandinavian Evangelical Church at Butte and Hoback, the Scandinavian Lutheran Church at 12th and Idaho, and the First German Methodist Episcopal Church at Prospect and Hoback. These are today private residences. Across from St. Helena's at Ninth and Hoback, the House of the Good Shepherd offered sanctuary to "wayward girls" who wished to rehabilitate. The complex included a dormitory, sisters' convent, and adjacent chapel (pictured here) in use from 1890 to 1909.

(Courtesy of the State Historic Preservation Office)

"First came the miners to work in the mines, then came the ladies to live on the line," sang early-day residents of the gold camps. Like all mining camps, Helena boasted a thriving restricted district. The women of the line worked out of small cabins abandoned by the first miners along Clore (now Park) Street from Reeder's Alley north for several blocks. By 1892, brick brothels replaced cabins to the right of the Pioneer Cabin, center, pictured here in 1933. (Montana Historical Society 954-125)

By the late 1880s, wealthy proprietor madams invested in property along Wood Street, linking with the old "line" on Clore Street to form an L-shaped district. Circa 1918, Joliet Street ends at the Bluestone House (center right with the dome). Deed records show that this landmark, designed by James Stranahan, was begun in 1889 as the private home of madam Lillie McGraw whose maison de joie was at its immediate foot. Lillie lost her fortune and the house was long unfinished. Mollie Byrnes' "The Castle" is kitty-corner from Lillie's. The district is pictured here circa 1918. (Uncatalogued Helena Collection)

Left and below: Mollie Byrnes built her own residence at 212 State Street, near but just outside the district, in 1890. She reputedly wanted to live in a respectable neighborhood but close enough to her business to find her way home after too much partying. Twice married, Mollie's desire for respectability ended with her death in 1899 of acute alcoholism. The cluttered 1890s interior of her home reflects Victorian era tastes.

(Left: Montana Historical Society PAc 85-9; below: contemporary of 212 State Street, Dave Shors photograph)

Right: Prohibition and federal and state reforms during WWI dispersed red light activities in Helena. By the 1930s, the district resurfaced in upstairs rooming houses along South Main Street. Whoever posed baby Pearl Maxwell must have had a premonition because Pearl grew up to become a well-known madam and proprietor of the Royal Rooms above the Boston Block from 1933 to 1953. (Crystal Wong Shors Collection)

Below: Longtime madam Ida Levy, who ran the house above the present-day Windbag Saloon and Grill, retired to Florida in the 1950s. "Big Dorothy" Baker took over the business and eventually owned three adjoining properties. Her back entrance pictured here was reputedly the best-known door in Helena.

(Uncatalogued Montana Historical Society Helena Urban Renewal Collection)

Left: In 1972 as downtown buildings crumbled and decayed around her, Dorothy Baker applied for a $500 federal urban renewal grant to fix up her property. She received the grant, but too much attention came with it and authorities closed her business. Dorothy, pictured in her younger years, died suddenly a few weeks before she had her day in court.

(Montana Historical Society PAc 80-5)

Most Prized Of The Lot

Schools and Youth Activities

Helena is justly proud of her schools, setting an example to be followed throughout
the territory. . . . No public architectural
features are more marked and distinct than
its school buildings, seven of which dot the
surface of the city's limits. "Central" [is]
probably the oldest and most familiar. . . .
Though not possessing the modern style. . .
or being as handsome as some of its com-
panion buildings, its early associations
make it the most prized of the lot.

Helena Board of Trade, 1889

The location of Helena's first public school (pictured right), noted in an 1892 story in the *Herald*, was 28 South Rodney: "The first public school in Helena was taught in a one-story board structure on the site now occupied by M. Reinig's residence." (The site today is the parking lot of St. John's Building.) The *Herald* went on to say that it "wasn't much of a schoolhouse, but an average of 100 scholars found it the best schoolhouse in the state, and the two teachers contrived to impart a deal of information to those who were willing to learn. There was only one room, with a teacher at each end; the boys on one side, and the girls on the other. The playground was the street, and the bell was perched on four posts at the rear of the building." A more substantial brick schoolhouse (above) replaced it.

(Grace V. Erickson photographs, Montana Historical Society 953-700 and 953-701)

A Harsh Lesson

Mary Sheehan Ronan attended Helena's first private school, a log cabin at Rodney and Broadway. She and her schoolmate, Sallie Davenport, each wrote of an incident that made a great impression on the young students. As they arrived at school one morning, from the schoolyard the children had a clear view down the hill to Dry Gulch near the head of State and Davis streets. There, dangling from a branch on the Hangman's Tree, was the limp form of a man. The boys ran up and down the gulch at every opportunity during recess, speculating about the "bad man" who received such awful punishment. The children were all distressed, and Mary recalled in her memoirs, "I hated the talk. It made me shiver.... that dreadful, pitiful object, with bruised head, disarrayed vest and trousers, with boots so stiff, so worn, so wrinkled, so strangely the most poignant of all the gruesome details. I tried to forget, but I have never forgotten. I have heard the story told, but for its truth I will not vouch, that one over-zealous Sunday school teacher marched her class to the foot of the tree for a close-up view of this horrible example of the results of a wayward life, hoping to frighten her young charges into paths of righteousness."

Helena High School, foreground, and old Central School, background, are pictured. Construction of old Central School began in 1875. Nick Kessler furnished 350,000 bricks for the building and the low bid for the project was $17,250. The cornerstone for Helena High was laid on Oct. 25, 1890, but the building wasn't finished until January 1893. In the winter of 1892, the *Helena Herald* lamented that the school would be completed some day, "perhaps in time for the grandchildren of the present scholars to attend school in it."

(Montana Historical Society 953-719)

Imagine This!

Central School, the first graded school in Montana Territory, opened in January 1876. Its construction entailed partial removal of Helena's first cemetery, which covered the hilltop overlooking the city. Many graves were removed to the new cemetery on Benton Avenue, but not all of them. Imagine making this discovery, reported by the *Herald* on April 14, 1893, on the way to school: "A slide of many tons of earth came down from the south side of the Lawrence Street cut last night. The fall of earth was from that part of the Central school grounds used many years ago as a burial plot, and the cave-off exposes the coffin in which lie the remains of some early-day resident. The sideboard carried away exposes the body, which is that of a person dressed in the garb of an early-day miner. The features are well-preserved and the hair and whiskers grown long, are decidedly red."

Left: John C. Paulsen designed the magnificent high school, finally completed in 1893 on the southwest corner of Warren and Lawrence streets. Its lofty entrance hall featured impressive columns and a double stairway. (Montana Historical Society 953-747)

Below: This 1884 musical group with Professor Peterman includes some notable Helena family names, including: 1st row—Harry Walker, Rhuling Parchen, Fred Kuphal; 2nd row—Bill Pope, Henry Parchen, (unidentified), Abe Silverman; 3rd row—Albert Parchen, unidentified boy, Asa Fisk, Prof. Peterman, Peterman boy, (unidentified) and Albert Raleigh. A decade later, steps were being taken at the high school to organize a 12-piece marching band and the school board announced that it would provide "condemned guns" for the cadets to use at their drills.

(Montana Historical Society 953-759)

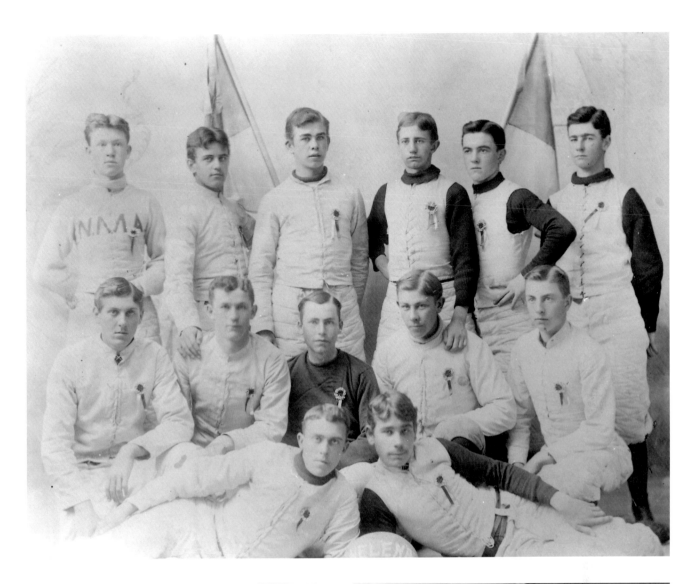

Above: Football took the lead as team sports were growing in popularity during the last decade of the 19th Century. The first semblance of a local sports page appeared in the *Helena Herald* in November of 1890. The Helena High School football team of 1894 proudly sported orange and purple jerseys, and included back row: C. Whitley, W. Wardman, G. McGaffery, Tom Hauser, P. Sullivan, Charles Curtis; front row: Theodore Lane, Alex Goodman, George Shaw, Charles Fisk and Charles Adams; lying in front: F. Ackley and Frank Gilpatrick.

(Montana Historical Society 953-769)

Right: A group of budding scientists posed "old bones" from the Helena High science lab as a teacher giving a lecture, circa 1893.

(Edward Reinig photograph, Montana Historical Society PAc 74-104.256)

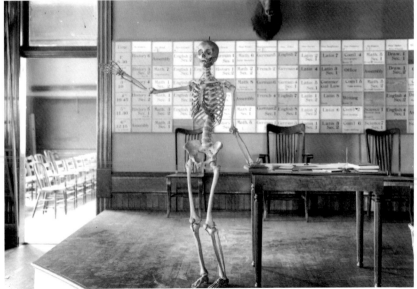

Left: Edward Reinig captured the "birdhouse gang" with their shop projects behind Central School in this undated photograph. (Montana Historical Society PAc 74-104.292)

Below: The basement of the Public Auditorium at 7th and Warren served as a classroom for kindergartners, and its lawn was their playground in 1912. (Montana Historical Society 953-699)

Bottom: Early school blackboard exercises included writing, art, math and geography. (Montana Historical Society 953-797)

Left: School children salute the flag in front of Helena High School in this May 10, 1898, Arbor Day photograph. (C. F. Pearis photograph, Montana Historical Society 953-723)

Above: Geometry and trigonometry were offered to third year students at Helena High at the turn of the century. A geometry class focuses front and center in this 1893 photograph. (Montana Historical Society 953-750)

Below: A series of photographs prepared for an exhibit at the Columbian Exposition, 1893, proudly shows off a recently completed Helena High School at the corner of Warren and Lawrence streets. Students pictured here were hard at work in the Art Department. (Montana Historical Society 953-748)

Helena High offered a broad spectrum of classes in the sciences and letters. The turn-of-the-century curriculum for third-year students included zoology, chemistry, physics, English, English literature and studies of Virgil. Extracurricular activities included an interest in drama. The 1899 class play was "The Rivals." Cast members included, left to right, Lloyd Gans, Joe Aldoron, George Odarue, Joe Rollins, Howard Cox, Vic Kessler, Ed Butcher, Edith Harrah, Lillian Lissner, Bea Shaffer and Martha Swan. (Montana Historical Society 953-767)

Members of the Helena High Orchestra pose for a formal portrait in 1907. (Montana Historical Society 953-762)

The 1923 Helena High girls basketball team played two games that year, both against Deer Lodge—home and away. "Basket Ball" is mentioned in the *Herald* for the first time in February 1900, stating that the busiest people in Helena were members of the senior class at Helena High School, who were preparing for "the game, the reception of the visitors, and the senior 'spread' to be given this evening in honor of the Bozeman visitors." The game was between the girls' teams and was played in the City Auditorium at 2 in the afternoon. Bozeman won the first half of the game by a score of 4 to 1. The ball used was larger than the Helena team had been accustomed to, and the local team was therefore handicapped, the *Herald* alibied. Miss Florence Fisk, captain of the Helena team, was taken sick at the close of the first half, which delayed the game for some time. Helena won the second half 9 to 7. (Montana Historical Society 953-770)

A Sea Of Seething Flames

Disasters

...on January 9, 1874 at about six-forty-five in the morning, as Mass neared its close, Father J. B. Palladino, S. J., pastor, turned and urged the sisters to hurry out and protect the buildings. A sea of seething flames was mounting Catholic Hill from the direction of Wood and upper Main Streets. Wind-driven sparks and cinders, flaming shingles, and live brands fell thick as snowflakes. The church, rectory, academy, and hospital caught fire several times, but the Sisters, pumping water from the wells, drenched each new blaze as it started and soaked roofs to prevent total loss.

Sister Julia Gilmore, *We Came North*

Left: Helena's survival despite fires, floods, and earthquakes is evidence that early settlers planted deep roots. Frame and log buildings built close together made fire a dangerous enemy. Even the fire tower itself burned several times. By 1871 six fire districts had been laid out and a corresponding number of rings on the fire bell, installed on Tower Hill, announced the fire's location. Today's Guardian of the Gulch, constructed in 1874 using millwright techniques, was the third such structure on Tower Hill. (Dave Shors photograph)

Below: Beginning in 1876, Helena firemen used this hose reel by pulling it to the scene of the fire. By 1879 two such reels, a rotary steam engine, and a hook and ladder truck were standard equipment. A watchman was on duty in the fire tower from dark to daylight and a patrol walked the streets for telltale signs of fire.

(E. H. Train photograph, Montana Historical Society 953-489)

By 1875 when these four members of the volunteer fire department were photographed, Helena had survived at least five major conflagrations. Left to right are A. J. Davidson, Charles Jeffers, Seth Bullock, T. H. Kleinschmidt.

(Montana Historical Society 953-487)

Fire wasn't the only natural disaster to strike Helena. In 1876, rupture of the Chessman Dam at Rimini caused $50,000 in damages and claimed three lives. In 1878 a freak cloudburst inundated Main Street, damaging precious supplies. "A flat-boat could have navigated down Broadway," claimed the *Herald*. A muddy Main Street pictured here shows the aftermath of a somewhat less serious cloudburst in 1880.

(Montana Historical Society PAc 80-27.f12)

Left: The obvious symbolism of the Atlas Block, completed in 1889, was not lost on old timers who witnessed the early conflagrations first-hand. Built by insurance company owner Samuel J. Jones, the landmark building served as a bold advertisement and reminder of past disasters. Stylized flames lick at the cornice while mythical salamander-like creatures, immune to fire, play at the top. Atlas, representing the insurance company, bears the burden. (Montana Historical Society 953-161)

Below: Helena firemen pose with their matched team and new wagon circa 1890. (Montana Historical Society PAc-80-27.f15)

Above: Firemen play pool in the main station at State and Main streets circa 1910. From left to right are William Hay, Martin Juhl, Cliff Hughes, Arthur Woods, Pat McKinnon, unidentified, Eddie Murphy, Charles Healy, John Nilan, Sid Boone, an unidentified news reporter, and Ed Guthrie.

(Montana Historical Society 953-499)

Right: The Helena Fire Department at Station No. 2 on Spruce (now Holter) Street between Madison and Harrison used this horse-drawn hose cart circa 1900.

(Arthur Canning photograph, Montana Historical Society 953-494)

Above: When 14-year-old Harry Anderson set fire to some burlap sacks on the top floor of the Montana Club in 1903, he only wanted to help the firemen put the fire out. But there was too much wind, too little water power, and no ladder high enough to reach the building's top floor. Ironically, the first floor offices of the water company and an insurance company were a total loss, too. Only the arches remained to be reused in the current Montana Club.

(Montana Historical Society 953-327)

Left: The Helena Hotel was Montana's premier hostelry from 1890, housing legislators during the first ground-breaking sessions immediately following statehood. Rooms cost an exorbitant $3 and up. Fire destroyed the building on February 4, 1912.

(Montana Historical Society 953-438)

Above: Lightning sparked a $1.5 million fire in 1928 that razed six business blocks along North Last Chance Gulch including the Gold Block, the Granite Block, the Bailey Block, and the New York Store leaving a blackened ruin in the center of the business district. As it had done before, Helena rebuilt. (Edward Reinig photograph, Montana Historical Society 953-473)

Right: On January 9, 1944, another devastating blaze destroyed the Montana Bank Building at Main and Edwards streets. L. H. Jorud photographed the icicles among the ruins. (Montana Historical Society 953-482)

Below: Most devastating of all disasters, however, were the earthquakes that rocked the area in October 1935, causing an estimated $4.5 million damage and claiming four lives. The children at St. Joseph's Home were left without a place to sleep, so the sisters made beds for them on the straw in a barn. (L. H. Jorud, photograph, IR file photo)

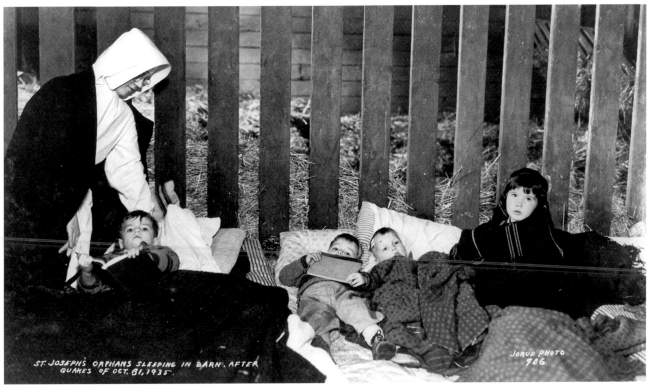

Left: **This building on South Main Street was the site of one fatality.**

(L. H. Jorud, photograph, IR file photo)

Shake, Rattle and Roll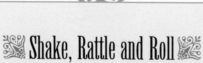

Humor came out of Helena's 1935 earthquakes, proving Queen City citizens a resilient bunch of folks who could pick up the pieces and even see the brighter side during adversity. C. R. Anderson (then principal at Broadwater and Hawthorne schools) told a story of how two cars were traveling toward each other 17 miles outside Helena. The river was on one side of the road and a steep cliff on the other. The cars were a short distance apart when a major temblor sent huge boulders and dirt onto the roadway between them. There was nothing to be done except exchange keys and cars—which they did—and each went on his way. It was said that hunters noticed that ducks flying in the vicinity preferred to take the long way around Helena. They would approach, circle and exclaim, "Quake, quake," and fly on. The earthquake changed the face of Helena, but strengthened the community. After the dust had settled, word went 'round that Helena had been renamed Lena, not because it leaned but because during those darkest hours, earthquakes knocked the "Hel" out of it.

Above: Boulder Hot Springs housed the children from St. Joseph's Home in the weeks following the disaster. Children board the bus at the Cathedral Rectory to travel to their temporary quarters at the resort. (L. H. Jorud, photograph, IR file photo)

Below: The new Helena High School (now Helena Middle School) was badly damaged and for weeks after the quakes, students attended classes in railroad cars. Students in this Related Science class, photographed in December of 1935, were more comfortable in the chilly car with their coats on. (L. H. Jorud, photograph, IR file photo)

Above: Earthquake repairs are still evident around town, as shown here in the replacement bricks in the upper level of the former Union Station, now the offices of Montana Rail Link. (Dave Shors photograph)

None Can Compare

"In all the northwest there is no place so beautiful. Of all the health resorts in America there is none which can compare in hygienic and chemical values [nor] a more perfectly appointed or a better equipped hostelry. . . . It may have been 16 years ahead of its time, but the 16 years have passed and its time has come."

Congressman Joseph Dixon, later Governor of Montana, upon the 1908 reopening of the Broadwater Hotel.

Right: Charles A. Broadwater had grandiose plans for the resort that he believed would bring prestige, visitors and income to the Helena community. Upon completion in 1889, an immense indoor plunge, beautiful grounds, elegant suites, elaborate furnishings, electric lights and sumptuous dining featuring ten-course meals seemingly gave the Broadwater all it needed to become a self-sustaining resort. The hotel, however, failed to draw non-resident visitors and was never the lucrative enterprise Broadwater had hoped. (Montana Historical Society 945-722)

Below: The Natatorium was an exotic Moorish style landmark housing the world's largest indoor "swimming bath." Several generations of Helenans fondly remember the special allure of the Broadwater, where families came for summer concerts and outings. The plunge remained the major attraction until 1935 when earthquakes irreparably damaged the structure and its wooden pipes. E. Louis Kracaw, left, and Mrs. Kracaw (in the black dress) enjoyed an outing in 1895.

(Cowan photograph, Montana Historical Society 945-810)

Above: The Broadwater required diverse employees including clerks, bookkeepers, cooks, waiters, housekeepers, groundskeepers, stable attendants, medical personnel and bathhouse attendants. The laundry alone, pictured in the 1890s, employed a small army.

(E. D. Keller and Arthur Canning photograph, Montana Historical Society 945-789)

Right: Today the 45-foot cupola, clearly visible from the interstate, is central to Reber Broadwater Cupola Park on Helena's eastern edge. Below: The seasonal nature of the resort business and the hotel's high maintenance limited the Broadwater's success. Gambling was a later focus until a crackdown on gaming closed the hotel for good in 1941. The natatorium was razed in 1946 and the old hotel in 1974. Scattered pieces and parts now decorate Helena homes and yards.

(Right, Dave Shors photograph; below, Montana Historical Society PAc 80-27)

John Ming built Helena's fabulous opera house on North Jackson Street, renowned throughout the Pacific Northwest, in 1880. European-style circular seating accommodated 1,000 while 62 state-of-the-art gas jets lit the stage. The upstairs housed Helena's first city hall offices in 1881. Today an impressive 1915 facade hides the original brick. Now the building serves as the Consistory Shrine Temple, where the public can view the Ming's original hand painted scenery used annually for the Masons' Easter Tableau.

(Montana Historical Society 953-834)

Several theatres showed "moving pictures," among them the Ming Opera House was one of the first in the early twentieth century. Later, the Marlow and the Rio at 335 North Main pictured here in 1936, offered movie-goers the latest on the big screen.

(Edward Reinig photograph, Montana Historical Society PAc 74-104)

A Pilgrim to this Town

When first a Pilgrim to this town I came—
A very fresh and tender-footed dame—
A Bridge street cabin was the only stage
Where Farce could roar, or Tragedy could rage:
An earthen floor, the sides of unhewn logs,
We charged for men—admittance free
    for dogs—
Where tender love scenes in the tragic lay
Were interrupted by the pack mule's bray,
And the prima donna's warble clear
On the high "C" and upper register,
Was ruined by the Sunday auctioneer.

Katie Putnam, actress
Ming Opera House dedication, 1880

Left: Helenans still mourn the demise of the Marlow Theatre, lost to urban renewal along with more than 200 historic buildings. Officials judged the theater unstable, but it took a mighty effort to finally bring it down in 1972. (IR file photo)

Below: August R. Schopfer (in the bowler hat) and other patrons enjoy their drafts at the Exchange Saloon, 101 S. Main. Many of Helena's 61 saloons in 1905 were elaborately outfitted with beautiful back bars, tin ceilings, and brass spittoons. The Exchange, along with other drinking establishments, closed upon Prohibition in 1918.

(Montana Historical Society 953-154)

It is hard to guess whether or not the horse was a regular at this watering hole.

(Edward Reinig photograph, Montana Historical Society PAc 74-104.334)

Above: These unidentified gentlemen, possibly soldiers at Fort Harrison, relax against a wall of lovely ladies proving that boys could decorate their rooms, too.

(Edward Reinig photograph, Montana Historical Society PAc 74-104.170)

Right: From the beginning East Helena was a company town. Asarco not only provided the paycheck, but was active in supporting family activities and sporting events. A small lake, created in 1899 by a dam on Prickly Pear Creek southeast of the plant, supplied cooling water for the smelter. But the same lake was popular for boating, fishing and swimming in the summer and ice skating in the winter. Called Lake Whitley after Charles W. Whitley, Asarco plant manager, it eventually filled with sediment. In 1900, with Whitley still manager, Asarco employed 600 men and a $100,000 expansion was also in the works that would require the employment of another 400 workers.

(A. H. Schenk photograph, Montana Historical Society PAc 80-27.f15)

Right: Whether for recreation or out of necessity, gardens flourished in back-yards and unused spaces and many Helenans were adept at horticulture.

(Edward Reinig photograph,
Montana Historical Society PAc 74-104.259)

Below: Anxious for a nice day in the snow, Helenans by the score hop onto the ski train to Blossburg at the Northern Pacific Depot, circa 1934.

(Montana Historical Society PAc 94-75.f20)

Above: Hunting and fishing were pastimes most young men grew up enjoying with their grandfathers, fathers, uncles and friends. Edward Reinig (at right) set his camera and took this photograph of himself and three companions. (Montana Historical Society PAc 74-104.275)

Left: Young Tom Judge, pictured in his boyhood cowboy outfit, went on to become governor of Montana, serving two terms from 1973 to 1981. Edward Reinig, Tom's great uncle, took the photograph.

(Montana Historical Society PAc 74-104.131)

Zest To Living

Celebrations

How I loved Helena! I loved its setting, high in the valley of the Prickly Pear. I loved its narrow, crooked Main Street that followed the course of Last Chance Gulch a little way and broke off abruptly in a wilderness. I loved the cross streets that led up and down steep hills and ended suddenly against other steeper hillsides, in prospect holes or in piles of tailings. It did not matter that the thoroughfares were trampled deep with dust or churned oozy with muddy long strings of mules, oxen, or horses drawing heavy wagons. . . . I was unaware of the ugliness of the hastily constructed frame and log buildings with false fronts and rickety porches. . . . I continued as in Virginia City to be neither curious about Helena's vices nor interested in their blatant demonstrations. The dry, light, sparkling air of the place invigorated me and gave zest to living.

Mary Ronan, *Frontier Woman: The Story of Mary Ronan as told to Margaret Ronan*

Left: E. H. Train photographed a Fourth of July parade on Broadway, in the late 1870s. The Federal Assay Office on Broadway is left, the Methodist Episcopal Church, replaced in the late 1880s, is on the right.
(Montana Historical Society 953-598)

Below: Flags flew on this 4th of July float as it moved past the apartment house on the southwest corner of Breckenridge and Rodney streets.
(Montana Historical Society 953-606)

Above: The congregation gathered under umbrellas on a wet October in 1891 as elders laid the cornerstone for the First Presbyterian Church at 11th Avenue and Ewing. The Temple Emanu-El in the center background had been dedicated the previous spring. The first Jewish synagogue in Montana, it now belongs to the Catholic Church, housing the offices of the Diocese of Helena.

(Arthur Canning photograph, Montana Historical Society 953-250)

Right: Fourth of July, 1902, people thronged Main Street to get the best view of the horse-drawn floats.

(Taylor Studio photograph, Montana Historical Society 953-614)

On July 3, 1908, Helena began a three-day Lewis and Clark Carnival in remembrance of the Corps of Discovery's trek through Montana. A huge arch decorated the intersection of Main and Sixth Avenue, and flags flew. This children's pageant was the first of many themed parades that wound their way beneath the arch over the course of the three-day celebration. The children's patriotic march featured fifteen hundred school children dressed in red, white and blue.

(Edward Reinig photograph, Montana Historical Society PAc 74-104.4)

Lewis and Clark, After the Fact

When Helenans make up their minds to celebrate, they do it right. On the heels of the Lewis and Clark Centennial, which the country technically celebrated from 1903 to 1906, Montana realized the moment had passed. Never mind. Helena hosted a carnival in 1907 that was so successful a much larger event was planned for 1908. The *Helena Independent* noted that the Lewis and Clark Carnival "was not a Helena affair, but was in commemoration of an event in which the entire northwest [was] interested." The city hired the country's leading costumers to help design a series of pageants authentically recreating the Expedition and other events dear to Montana. At the start of the celebration, the 45-member Expedition arrived, properly outfitted, amidst great fanfare. Another event featured Alder Gulch discoverer Henry Edgar, at 80, driving a vintage bullet-scarred stagecoach. There was a Carnival Chorus, athletic events at Haymarket Square, and revelry throughout the city. People came

from all over the state. Helena had not seen such celebrating since the town was crowned capital in 1894. During the three-day event, said the *Independent*, "All class lines were erased and pauper and millionaire went up and down the streets of the city celebrating in the same way…."

The most unique feature of the event was a surprise "Ghost Parade" given by the Montana Club at midnight on July 4th. Members appeared in ghost masks and pure white garments with skulls and cross bones painted over them. The procession went slowly up Main Street as the state capital band played a dirge. It was a weird scene. When the marchers reached a certain point, the band suddenly burst into its liveliest music. The "ghosts" ripped off their masks, dancing, singing, and cheering. There were still plenty of party-goers afoot at three A.M. to witness balloons with firecrackers inside ascend into the night sky and explode as they traveled overhead.

Above: Young ladies riding sidesaddle, young men on foot, and a flower bedecked carriage line up for a parade in front of the Cruse mansion at Lawrence and Benton Avenue.
(Montana Historical Society PAc 80-27.f13)

Right: Flower parades were a tradition and Helenans like this young lady, sitting sidesaddle on a blanket of blooms, delighted spectators.
(Edward Reinig photograph,
Montana Historical Society PAc 74-104.351)

Left: A fine carriage ready for the parade, its driver in formal livery and team trimmed in blossoms, awaits the signal to begin.
(Edward Reinig photograph, Montana Historical Society PAc 74-104.241)

Below: When Robinson Circus camels paraded along Helena's streets in 1890, bystanders marveled at the strange creatures. But a few old timers remembered that it wasn't the first time these exotic animals created a spectacle downtown. In 1865, camel trains delivered flour and other staples to Helena and other Montana mining camps.
(Montana Historical Society 953-277)

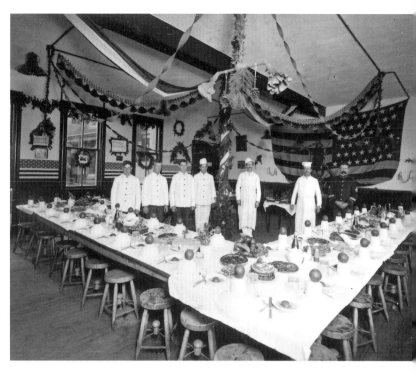

Right: Cooks and servers stand proudly at a special Christmas dinner prepared at Fort Harrison in 1907. The men outdid themselves setting a sumptuous table complete with fruit resting on inverted coffee cups. The establishment of Fort William Henry Harrison here in the 1890s was somewhat controversial. Despite objections from Missoula's Board of Trade, whose members feared a new military post in Helena would spell the ruin of Fort Missoula, construction began in 1893 on 1,040 acres known as the Kessler site. The first two buildings completed in the spring of 1895 were the guardhouse and the blacksmith shop. That fall the first soldiers, two companies of the 22nd Infantry at Fort Assinniboine, were ordered to Fort Harrison, which had been constructed at a cost of $214,000.
(Edward Reinig photograph, Montana Historical Society PAc 74-104.356)

Below: Camaraderie among men in assorted uniforms, and their dogs, made the holiday special for these soldiers at Fort Harrison in 1907. (Edward Reinig photograph, Montana Historical Society PAc 74-104.2)

Above: William Howard Taft was one of six sitting presidents to visit Helena. Taft, along with James J. Hill, opened the Seventh Annual Montana State Fair on Sept. 27, 1909, to an enthusiastic crowd estimated to be 10,000 strong. He also assisted Bishop Carroll in laying the cornerstone of the new Catholic college being built on Capitol Hill.

(Davis photograph, Montana Historical Society 949-798)

Right: President William Howard Taft is shown speaking briefly to people as he toured Helena in an open vehicle during his 1909 visit. Other presidents who visited the Capital City were: Theodore Roosevelt, May 27, 1903; Woodrow Wilson, Sept. 11, 1919; Warren G. Harding, June 29, 1923; Harry Truman, May 12, 1950; and George Bush, Sept. 18, 1989.

(Davis, Capital Studio photograph, Montana Historical Society 949-803)

Ex-President Theodore Roosevelt visited Helena on April 12, 1911, and delivered his "sermon on good citizenship" from the steps of the Helena High School Building. Despite inclement weather he received an enthusiastic welcome and stayed in the Capital City 12 hours. "Ladies and Gentlemen: Naturally it is a rare and peculiar pleasure to be here as a guest of Montana and Helena," Roosevelt said. "I did not need any pressure to make me come to Montana and especially Helena. On the contrary, it would have taken pressure to have kept me away.... I find myself among friends whom I have known for many years, and while here, I feel more and more that the people of Montana and the west are the leaders of the future."

(S. J. Culbertson photographs, Montana Historical Society PAc 74-104.239 and PAc 74-104.238)

Left: The state's finest farm crops and produce were proudly displayed at the State Fair, Lewis and Clark County, in 1911. Helena hosted the first territorial fair in September 1870. It eventually became the state fair, which was hosted in Helena until August of 1932. (Montana Historical Society 949-869)

Below: A large crowd gathers as Bishop John Patrick Carroll consecrates the cornerstone for the Cathedral of St. Helena in 1908. The Cathedral was dedicated in 1914 and then consecrated in 1924 after all the stained glass windows were installed. (Courtesy of the Archives of the Diocese of Helena)

Monsignor Victor Day, a parish priest and administrator at the Cathedral of St. Helena, baptized a baby in this circa 1920 photo. Msgr. Day was named a parish assistant in Helena in 1894. He died in 1946.

(Edward Reinig photograph, Montana Historical Society PAc 74-104-285)

Edward Reinig captured this solemn vignette circa 1920. A young boy kneels in the confessional at the Cathedral of St. Helena in this circa 1920 photo as Monsignor Victor Day listens. (Montana Historical Society PAc 74-104-280)

Feel The Legacy

All you have to do is walk south on Main Street and you can feel the legacy stemming from the indomitable spirit of early day miners as they tried to scratch out a living.

Gerald Sullivan, *Helena '45*

Edward Reinig photographed this miner's cabin high in the mountains near Helena in the early twentieth century. Such cabins still dot the mountain slopes, melting back into the earth as a reminder that the community's roots are in mining, and these roots go deep.

(Montana Historical Society PAc 74-104.306)

What's in a Name?

State Street was originally called Bridge Street because Last Chance Creek ran along it and a small footbridge allowed pedestrians to cross. By 1890, the creek ran underground through a flume. The street had been Helena's first commercial area but by the 1880s it housed some unsavory businesses and saloons. The city council passed ordinances forcing some of them to move elsewhere. Remaining residents changed the name to State Street "unmindful," said the *Herald*, "that this would blot out its still earlier history." A similar name change occurred on Wood Street, the heart of the redlight district. Residents after the turn of the century wanted to erase the Wood Street stigma. The name was officially changed to Miller Street, after D. J. Miller, one of the so-called Four Georgians, in 1963. Citizens hardly remember the name of Capt. George Wood, who help lay out the townsite. Clore Street, the oldest section of Helena's redlight district, became Park Street in 1912.

Warren Street bears the name of Warren Toole and Ewing Street is named for General R. C. Ewing. George Wood named Joliet Street after his hometown of Joliet, Illinois. Breckenridge, Jackson, and Cutler streets were all named for early settlers, and many of the Sixth Ward streets are name for railroad officials. LeGrand Cannon Boulevard, often incorrectly identified as LeGrand Canyon, memorializes LeGrand Cannon, the son of Helena businessman C. W. Cannon.

Main Street became Last Chance Gulch at Christmas in 1953 because Helenans decided the quaint name would attract tourists.

Left: The U.S. Treasury Department built a federal assay office in Helena, one of five in the nation, where much of the great wealth that once came from Montana soil was melted and weighed. Under construction in 1875, the building at 200 E. Broadway is of national and regional significance as the first officially recorded federal building in Montana Territory. At far left in the photograph is a portion of the newly-completed Central School.
(E. H. Train photograph,
Montana Historical Society 953-877)

Below: When Shirley Ashby and Colonel Charles Broadwater built his substantial business block at 6th Avenue in 1883, it was the first this far north on Main Street. Many were skeptical of real estate investments so far removed from downtown, but by 1893 the Power Block, Electric Building and the Montana Club anchored the area that once held corrals, feed lots and a lumber mill. The First National Bank Building replaced it in 1930.
(Edward Reinig photograph, Montana Historical Society PAc 74-104.233)

Above: Helena at the turn of the twentieth century had an impressive skyline. Pictured prominently are the landmark Power Block, left, and the first elaborate Montana Club with the round tower. Behind it is the tall stack of the Electric Block, leased in 1891 to house the first legislative session after statehood, which supplied steam power to downtown. Many a dance was held in the Electric Block's huge ballroom.

(Montana Historical Society PAc 80-27.14)

Right: The Electric Block and the old Montana Club flank the Diamond Block.

(Montana Historical Society PAc 80-27.f14)

Colonel C. A. Broadwater's Montana National Bank, shown at left before remodeling in 1890, stood on the southwest corner of Main and Edwards. As the story goes, someone criticized Broadwater's lavish spending. Helena was not worth it, said the critic, since buffalo in time would again graze along the gulch. Soon enough, one did. Broadwater added a granite buffalo head over his bank's doorway. That landmark, above, now guards the entrance to the Lewis and Clark Library.

(Left, Montana Historical Society PAc 80-27.f15; above, Dave Shors, photograph)

Helena boasted a thoroughly cosmopolitan downtown in 1905. Looking north from Broadway to Sixth Avenue, the Montana National Bank, left, dominates the streetscape. The prominent dome of the First National Bank is left and the Ashby Block on the northwest corner of Sixth and Main is clearly visible.

(Edward Reinig photograph, Montana Historical Society PAc 74.104.336)